From Japanese To English

Copyright © 2016 by Ralph Duncans Jr.

From Japanese To English
Ralph Duncans Jr.

ISBN: 978-0-9961766-3-7

This is an English language-learning book.

Table Of Contents

Part One - Translating Japanese Questions

Translating Form of BE Questions..1
Translating Action Questions..3
Translating Modal Verbs' Questions...5

Part Two - Answering English Questions

Making Questions - BE Verbs..7
Answering Questions - Form of BE Verbs...8
Making Questions - Action Verbs...9
Answering Questions - Action Verbs...10
Action Verbs: $(V^2) + (V^4) = (V^2 + V^4)$...11

Part Three - Speaking

Grammatical Structures..15

Part Four - Statements To Questions

Statements To Questions – Action Verbs..18

Part One
Translating Japanese Questions

Translating Form of BE Questions

$$(\sim)^1 + (v)^2 + (s)^3 + (\sim)^4 + ?$$

$$\# = \#$$
$$s = s$$
$$p = p$$

s = singular   p = plural

1. Who, what, when, where, why, which, how.

2. The verb – past, present, future.

3. The subject – singular or plural.

4. The rest of the question.

"be" = 1, 2, 3, 4 ~ ∞

Past Tense	Present Tense	Future Tense
(I) was = singular (s)	am = only I	will ~ be =
were = plural (p)	is = singular (s)	singular and plural
	are = plural (p)	
ありました	あります	~だろう
いました	います	あります
なりました	なります	います
でした	です	なります
		です

1

Translating Form of BE Questions

1. The question in Japanese.
2. Translate.
3. The order: 1, 3, 2, 4.
4. $\underbrace{}_{(\sim)^1}$ + $\underbrace{}_{\substack{(v)^2 \\ \#}}$ + $\underbrace{}_{\substack{(s)^3 \\ \#}}$ + $\underbrace{}_{(\sim)^4}$ + ?

   (with # = # under (v)² and (s)³)

5. The question in English.
6. Please check. (Nouns)
7. The final question in English.

Example

1. あなたはいえのなかにいますか。

2. <u>あなた</u>　<u>いえ</u>　<u>のなか</u>　<u>います</u>か。
   　you　　house　　in　　　be + <u>present tense</u>

   　　　　　　　　　　　　　　am = only I
   　　　　　　　　　　　　　　is = singular (s)
   　　　　　　　　　　　　　　are = plural (p)

   singular = 1
   plural = 2, 3, 4 ~ ∞

   a = 1, an = 1 (not special)
   the = 1, 2, 3, 4 ~ ∞ (special)

3. 1, 3, 2, 4.

4. $\underbrace{\sim}_{(\sim)^1}$ + $\underbrace{are}_{\substack{(v)^2 \\ p}}$ + $\underbrace{you}_{\substack{(s)^3 \\ p}}$ + $\underbrace{in\ house}_{(\sim)^4}$ + ?

   (with p = p under (v)² and (s)³)

5. Are you in house?
6. Are you in (a, ~~an~~, the) house?　　(a = not special)　(the = special)
7. Are you in the house? (special)　　or　　Are you in a house? (not special)

Nouns (名)

1. a noun = a person, a place, a thing
2. + s = plural (p)　　 - s = singular (s)

Translating Action Verbs' Questions

$$(\sim)^1 + (v)^2 + (s)^3 + (v)^4 + (\sim)^5 + ?$$

$$\# = \#$$
$$s = s$$
$$p = p$$

s = singular   p = plural

1. Who, what, when, where, why, which, how.

2. The verb – past, present, future.

3. The subject – singular or plural.

4. The verb – plural only.

5. The rest of the question.

Past Tense	Present Tense	Future Tense
did ~?	do ~?	will ~ do?
did = singular and plural	do = plural (p) does = singular (s)	will = singular and plural
～ました	～ます	～ だろう ～ます

3

Translating Action Verbs' Questions

1. The question in Japanese.
2. Translate.
3. The order: 1, 3, 2, 4, 5.
4. $\underset{(\sim)^1}{\underline{\hspace{1cm}}} + \underset{\underset{\#}{(v)^2}}{\underline{\hspace{1cm}}} + \underset{\underset{\#}{(s)^3}}{\underline{\hspace{1cm}}} + \underset{(v)^4}{\underline{\hspace{1cm}}} + \underset{(\sim)^5}{\underline{\hspace{1cm}}} + ?$

   $\# = \#$

5. The question in English.
6. Please check. (Nouns)
7. The final question in English.

Example

1. あなたはそとでいすにすわりましたか。

   $(v)^2 \quad (v)^4$

2. <u>あなた</u>　<u>そと</u>　<u>いす</u>　<u>に</u>　<u>すわり</u><u>ました</u>か。
   You　　outside　chair　in　　sit　　past tense

   singular = 1
   plural = 2, 3, 4 ~ ∞
   a = 1, an = 1 (not special)
   the = 1, 2, 3, 4 ~ ∞ (special)
   did = singular and plural

3. 1, 3, 2, 4, 5.

4. $\underset{(\sim)^1}{\underline{\sim}} + \underset{\underset{p}{(v)^2}}{\underline{did}} + \underset{\underset{p}{(s)^3}}{\underline{you}} + \underset{(v)^4}{\underline{sit}} + \underset{(\sim)^5}{\underline{\text{in chair outside}}} + ?$

   $p = p$

5. Did you sit in chair outside?
6. Did you sit in (a, ~~an~~, the) chair outside? (a = not special) (the = special)
7. Did you sit in the chair outside?　or　Did you sit in a chair outside?

Nouns (名)
1. a noun = a person, a place, a thing
2. + s = plural (p)　　- s = singular (s)

Action verbs (動)
1. an action verb + s = singular (s)
2. an action verb - s = plural (p)

Translating Modal Verbs' Questions
(A Necessity or A Possibility)

must² - present tense only	shall² – present tense should² – past tense	will² – future tense would² – past tense

can² – present tense could² – past tense	may² – present tense might² – past tense

Action Verbs' Questions Formula
$(\sim)^1 + (v)^2 + (s)^3 + (v)^4 + (\sim)^5 + ?$

1. must - …なければならないですか。

    $(\sim)^1 + (must)^2 + (s)^3 + (v)^4 + (\sim)^5 + ?$

2. shall or should - …ましようか。…べきですか。

    $(\sim)^1 + (shall\ or\ should)^2 + (s)^3 + (v)^4 + (\sim)^5 + ?$

3. will or would - …だろうか。…するだろうか。…しただろうか。

    $(\sim)^1 + (will\ or\ would)^2 + (s)^3 + (v)^4 + (\sim)^5 + ?$

4. can or could - …できますか。…できましたか。

    $(\sim)^1 + (can\ or\ could)^2 + (s)^3 + (v)^4 + (\sim)^5 + ?$

5. may or might - …してもよいですか。…かもしれないですか。

    $(\sim)^1 + (may\ or\ might)^2 + (s)^3 + (v)^4 + (\sim)^5 + ?$

Note: All modal verbs are plural and singular.

Part Two
Answering English Questions

Yes, ___ + ___ .
     (s)³   (v)²   (~)⁴
    = ___ + ___

No, ___ + ___ + not + ___ .
    (s)³   (v)²   (~)⁴
   = ___ + ___

___ + ___ + ___ + ___ + ?
(~)¹   (v)²   (s)³   (~)⁴

Making Questions
BE Verbs

(~)¹	(v)²	(s)³	(~)⁴
Who		I	⎧ a ⎫
What		we	⎨ an ⎬ ~
When		you	⎩ the⎭
Where		he	
Why		she	
Which		it	
How		they	

1. **Past Tense**
   (I) was - s
       were - p

2. **Present Tense**
   am - only I
   is - singular
   are - plural

3. **Future Tense**
   will + ___ + be + ~
          (s)³   (~)⁴
   (v)²
   s and p

Q. You? A. I.
Q. I?   A. You.

Past Tense	Present Tense	Future Tense
ありました	あります	～だろう
いました	います	あります
なりました	なります	います
でした	です	なります
		です

Nouns (名)

1. a noun = a person, a place or a thing
2. a noun + s = plural (p)
   a noun − s = singular (s)

s = singular (1)
p = plural (2, 3, 4 ~ ∞)

a = 1, an = 1 (not special)
the = 1, 2, 3, 4 ~ ∞ (special)

the = my (私の), your (貴方の), our (私達の), his (彼の), her (彼女の), its (それの), their (彼らの, 彼女らの, それらの)

Answering Questions
Form of BE Verbs

1. The question in English.
2. Write the form of BE formula of the question under the question.

3. $\underset{(s)^3}{\text{_____}} + \underset{(v)^2}{\text{_____}} + \underset{(\sim)^4}{\text{_____}} + \underset{(\sim)^1}{\text{_____}}.$

4. Please check. (Nouns)
5. The final sentence.

Example: Where is the dog?

1. <u>Where</u>   <u>is</u>   <u>the dog</u>?
2. $(\sim)^1$ $(v)^2$ $(s)^3$

singular = 1
plural = 2, 3, 4 ~ ∞

a = 1, an = 1 (not special)

the = 1, 2, 3, 4 ~ ∞ (special)

3. $\underset{\substack{(s)^3 \\ \#}}{\underline{\text{The dog}}} + \underset{\substack{(v)^2 \\ =}}{\underline{\text{ is }}} + \underset{\substack{(\sim)^1 \\ \#}}{\underline{\text{in   house}}}$

4. The dog is in (a, ~~an~~, the) house.   (the = special)   (a = not special)

5. The dog is in the house.

Nouns (名)

1. a noun = a person, a place, a thing
2. + s = plural (p)   - s = singular (s)

Making Questions
Action Verbs

Yes, (s)³ + (v)² + (~)⁵.
= ___ + (v)² + (v)⁴ + ___

No, (s)³ + (v)² + not + (v)⁴ + (~)⁵.
= ___

(~)¹ + (s)³ + (v)⁴ + ?

(~)¹	(s)³	(v)⁴	(~)⁵
Who	I		a ⎫
What	we		an ⎬ ~
When	you		the ⎭
Where	he		
Why	she		
Which	it		
How	they	a plural action verb	

Q. You? A. I.
Q. I? A. You.

(v)²

1. Past Tense
   did – s and p

Past Tense	Present Tense	Future Tense
~ました	~ます	~だろう

2. Present Tense
   do – plural
   does – singular

   ~ます

3. Future Tense
   will – s and p

Nouns (名)
1. a noun = a person, a place or a thing
2. a noun + s = plural (p)
   a noun – s = singular (s)

Verbs (動)
1. an action verb + s = singular (s)
2. an action verb – s = plural (p)

s = singular (1)
p = plural (2, 3, 4 ~ ∞)

a = 1, an = 1 (not special)
the = 1, 2, 3, 4 ~ ∞ (special)

the = my (私の), your (貴方の), our (私達の), his (彼の), her (彼女の), its (それの), their (彼らの, 彼女らの, それらの)

9

Answering Questions
Action Verbs

1. The question in English.
2. Write the action verb formula of the question under the question.
3. $\underline{}_{(s)^3} + \underline{}_{(v)^2 + (v)^4} + \underline{}_{(\sim)^5} + \underline{}_{(\sim)^1}$.

4. Please check. (Nouns)
5. The final sentence.

___

Example: Where do you read a book?

1. $\underline{\text{Where}} \ \underline{\text{do}} \ \underline{\text{you}} \ \underline{\text{read}} \ \underline{\text{a book}}$?
2. $\ (\sim)^1 \quad (v)^2 \ \ (s)^3 \ \ (v)^4 \quad (\sim)^5$

singular = 1
plural = 2, 3, 4 ~ ∞

a = 1, an = 1 (not special)

the = 1, 2, 3, 4 ~ ∞ (special)

3. $\underline{\text{I}}_{(s)^3} + \underline{\text{read}}_{(v)^2 + (v)^4} + \underline{\text{a book}}_{(\sim)^5} + \underline{\text{in room}}_{(\sim)^1}$

4. I read a book in (a, ~~an~~, the) room.
5. I read a book in a room.

___

Nouns (名)
    1. a noun = a person, a place, a thing
    2. + s = plural (p)   - s = singular (s)

Action verbs (動)
    1. an action verb + s = singular (s)
    2. an action verb - s = plural (p)

Action Verbs: $(V^2) + (V^4) = (V^2 + V^4)$

Past (過去)	Present		Future
S & P	(I) P	S	S & P
V^2 = did	V^2 = do	V^2 = does	V^2 = will
~	V^4	~	~
~ + ed	~	~ + s	will ~
did	do	does	will do
ate	eat	eats	will eat
went	go	goes	will go
walked	walk	walks	will walk
played	play	plays	will play
ran	run	runs	will run
sat	sit	sits	will sit
drank	drink	drinks	will drink
wrote	write	writes	will write
stood	stand	stands	will stand
washed	wash	washes	will wash
brushed	brush	brushes	will brush
heard	hear	hears	will hear

$$(V^2) + V^4 = (V^2 + V^4)$$

$\dfrac{do}{(v)^2} + \dfrac{do}{(v)^4} = $ _____ $(v)^2 + (v)^4$

$\dfrac{did}{(v)^2} + \dfrac{hear}{(v)^4} = $ _____ $(v)^2 + (v)^4$

$\dfrac{does}{(v)^2} + \dfrac{go}{(v)^4} = $ _____ $(v)^2 + (v)^4$

$\dfrac{does}{(v)^2} + \dfrac{stand}{(v)^4} = $ _____ $(v)^2 + (v)^4$

$\dfrac{did}{(v)^2} + \dfrac{sit}{(v)^4} = $ _____ $(v)^2 + (v)^4$

$\dfrac{do}{(v)^2} + \dfrac{stand}{(v)^4} = $ _____ $(v)^2 + (v)^4$

$\dfrac{will}{(v)^2} + \dfrac{drink}{(v)^4} = $ _____ $(v)^2 + (v)^4$

$\dfrac{did}{(v)^2} + \dfrac{brush}{(v)^4} = $ _____ $(v)^2 + (v)^4$

$\dfrac{will}{(v)^2} + \dfrac{write}{(v)^4} = $ _____ $(v)^2 + (v)^4$

$\dfrac{will}{(v)^2} + \dfrac{wash}{(v)^4} = $ _____ $(v)^2 + (v)^4$

$\dfrac{does}{(v)^2} + \dfrac{run}{(v)^4} = $ _____ $(v)^2 + (v)^4$

$\dfrac{did}{(v)^2} + \dfrac{play}{(v)^4} = $ _____ $(v)^2 + (v)^4$

$\dfrac{do}{(v)^2} + \dfrac{walk}{(v)^4} = $ _____ $(v)^2 + (v)^4$

$\dfrac{does}{(v)^2} + \dfrac{eat}{(v)^4} = $ _____ $(v)^2 + (v)^4$

Action Verbs: $(V^2) + (V^4) = (V^2 + V^4)$

Past (過去)	Present		Future
S & P	(I) P	S	S & P
V^2 = did	V^2 = do	V^2 = does	V^2 = will
~	V^4	~	~
~ + ed	~	~ + s	will ~
did	do	does	will do
	throw		
	hide		
	breathe		
	cook		
			will talk
shopped			
thought		thinks	
			will drive
		rides	
	pull		
pushed			
			will study

Fill in the spaces with the correct grammatical forms.

Part Three
Speaking

Grammatical Structures

1. <u>Action Verbs (動) - eat</u>

   わたしは りんごを たべます。
   　I　　　 an apple　 eat/eats

   <u>special</u>　　<u>　　　</u>　　<u>　　　</u>
   　　1　　　　　3　　　　　2

   <u>I eat an apple.</u>

Action verbs

Past (過去)	Present		Future	Perfect (過分)
S and P	(I) P	S	S and P	---------
~ + ed	~	~ + s	will ~	---------
ate	eat	eats	will eat	eaten
ました	～ます		だろう, ～ます	

2. <u>BE Verbs</u>

   りんごが あかい です。
   The apple red   present + be
   <u>　s　</u>　<u>　　</u>　<u>am/is/are</u>
   　1　　　 3　　　　2

   <u>The apple is red.</u>

BE Verbs

Past (過去)	Present	Future
(I) was = s were = p	am = only I is = singular are = plural	will be
ありました, いました なりました, でした	あります, います, なります, です	だろう, あります, います, なります, です

3. <u>BE verbs and Present Participles</u>

   ～しています - ～ + ing (現分)

   わたしはりんごを たべて　 います。
   <u>　I　</u>　<u>an apple</u>　<u>eating</u>　<u>am/is/are</u>
   　1　　　4　　　　3　　　　2

   <u>I am eating an apple.</u>

<u>Nouns (名)</u>

1. a noun = a person, a place, a thing
2. + s = plural (p)　- s = singular (s)
3. I = special

4. (a) Present and (b) Past Perfect Tense　a. ～したこと　があります b. ～したこと　がありました
   　　have/has　　 had　過分　　　　　過分　　have/has　 過分　　　had

   a. わたしはりんごをたべたことがあります。
   　<u>　I　</u>　<u>an apple</u>　<u>eaten</u>　<u>have/has</u>
   　　1　　　4　　　　3　　　　2

   <u>I have eaten an apple.</u>

   b. わたしはりんごを<u>たべたこと</u> がありました。
   　<u>　I　</u>　<u>an apple</u>　<u>eaten</u>　<u>had</u>
   　　1　　　4　　　　3　　　　2

   <u>I had eaten an apple.</u>

singular = 1

plural = 2, 3, 4 ~ ∞

a = 1, an = 1 (not special)

the = 1, 2, 3, 4 ~ ∞ (special)

I　He		me　him
You　She		you　her
We　It		us　it
They	verb	them
(s)	(v)	(~)

5. <u>There I am/There is/There are (がある／がいる).</u>

   b. <u>あかいりんごがあります。</u>
   　<u>a red apple</u>　<u>There is</u>
   　　　2　　　　　1

   a. There I am eating an apple.

There { I
he, she, it
you, we, they } { am
is
are } .

b. There is a red apple.

Grammatical Structures

6. Passive Voice/Respect

$$\underline{\sim\ に}\quad \underline{\sim}\quad \underline{られ}\quad \underline{(ます／ました)}$$
by　　　過分　　　be　　　present/past

I eat an apple.

りんごは	わたし	に	たべ	られ	ます。
an apple	me	by	eaten	be + present	
				am/is/are	
s					
1	5	4	3	2	

An apple is eaten by me.

7. Causative-Respective

$$\underline{\sim\ に}\quad \underline{\sim}\ +\ \underline{させ}\ +\ \underline{られ}\ +\ \underline{(ます／ました)}$$
by　　　to ~　　　made　　　be　　　present/past

私は	友達	に	りんご を	たべ	させ	られ	ます。
I	a friend	by	an apple	to eat	made	be + present	
						am/is/are	
special	s		s				
1	7	6	5	4	3	2	

I am made to eat an apple by a friend.

8. Causative

$$\underline{\sim\ に}\ +\ \underline{\sim}\ +\underline{たべ}+\ \underline{させ}\ +\ \underline{(ます／ました)}$$
　　　　　　　　eat　　make　　present/past

私 は	友達に	りんご を	食べ	させ	ます。
I	a friend	an apple	eat	make + present	
				make/makes	
special	s	s			
1	3	5	4	2	

I make a friend eat an apple.

Part Four
Statements to Questions

Statements To Questions
(Action Verbs)

1. "Yes." or "No." = (~)¹?
2. ~~"Yes."~~ or ~~"No."~~ = (~)¹?

(~)¹
who, what, when, where,
why, which, how

$$\underline{\quad}_{(\sim)^1} + \underline{\quad}_{(v)^2} + \underline{\quad}_{(s)^3} + \underline{\quad}_{(v)^4} + \underline{\quad}_{(\sim)^5} + ?$$

s, p = s, p

---

who	does	where	what	which	*what
He	walks	to the store	to the store	to the store	to the store.
$(s)^3$	$(v^2 + v^4)$	$(\sim)^{1,5}$	$(\sim)^{1,5}$	$(\sim)^{1,5}$	$(\sim)^{1,5}$
s	= s				

---

who
He walks to the store.
$(s)^3$ (v^2+v^4) $(\sim)^{1,5}$

Who + walks + to the store + ?
$(\sim)^1$ $(v)^2$ + ~~$(s)^3$~~ + $(v)^4$ $(\sim)^5$
s = s

what
He walks to the store.
$(s)^3$ (v^2+v^4) $(\sim)^{1,5}$

What + does + he + walk + to + ?
$(\sim)^1$ $(v)^2$ $(s)^3$ $(v)^4$ $(\sim)^5$
s = s

where
He walks to the store.
$(s)^3$ (v^2+v^4) $(\sim)^{1,5}$

Where + does + he + walk + ?
$(\sim)^1$ (v) $(s)^3$ $(v)^4$
s = s

which
He walks to (the store).
$(s)^3$ (v^2+v^4) $(\sim)^{1,}$

Which store + does + he + walk + to + ?
$(\sim)^1$ $(v)^2$ $(s)^3$ $(v)^4$ $(\sim)^5$
s = s

***what**
He walks to the store.
$(s)^3$ (v^2+v^4) $(\sim)^{1,5}$

He + walks + to the *what + ?
$(s)^1$ $(v)^2 + (v)^4$ $(\sim)^5$
s = s

*This pattern is used mostly when the hearer/listener did not hear the noun or other words.

Note: BE verbs' questions are simple to make. Just omit $(v)^4$. Make sure to select the correct past and present tense BE verbs.

www.ingramcontent.com/pod-product-compliance
Lightning Source LLC
Chambersburg PA
CBHW040546020526
44113CB00057B/2771